AN IDEAS INTO ACTION GUIDEBOOK

Influence for Nonprofit Leaders

IDEAS INTO ACTION GUIDEBOOKS

Aimed at managers and executives who are concerned with their own and others' development, each guidebook in this series gives specific advice on how to complete a developmental task or solve a leadership problem.

LEAD CONTRIBUTOR	Deborah Friedman
CONTRIBUTORS	Gloria Bernabeu
	Shera Clark
	Karen Dyer
	Lynn Fick-Cooper
	Kelly M. Hannum
	Lyndon Rego
	Harold Scharlatt
	Bertrand Sereno
	Sandrine Tunezerwe
DIRECTOR OF ASSESSMENTS, TOOLS, AND PUBLICATIONS	Sylvester Taylor
MANAGER, PUBLICATION DEVELOPMENT	Peter Scisco
EDITORS	Stephen Rush, Karen Lewis
ASSOCIATE EDITOR	Shaun Martin
ASSISTANT EDITOR	Joan Bello
DESIGN AND LAYOUT	Joanne Ferguson
COVER DESIGN	Laura J. Gibson
	Chris Wilson, 29 & Company
RIGHTS AND PERMISSIONS	Kelly Lombardino

CCL No. 459
ISBN No. 978-1-60491-170-1

CENTER FOR CREATIVE LEADERSHIP
WWW.CCL.ORG

AN IDEAS INTO ACTION GUIDEBOOK

Influence for Nonprofit Leaders

Deborah Friedman

Center for
Creative
Leadership®

THE IDEAS INTO ACTION GUIDEBOOK SERIES

This series of guidebooks draws on the practical knowledge that the Center for Creative Leadership (CCL) has generated since its inception in 1970. The purpose of the series is to provide leaders with specific advice on how to complete a developmental task or solve a leadership challenge. In doing that, the series carries out CCL's mission to advance the understanding, practice, and development of leadership for the benefit of society worldwide.

CCL's unique position as a research and education organization supports a community of accomplished scholars and educators in a community of shared knowledge. CCL's knowledge community holds certain principles in common, and its members work together to understand and generate practical responses to the ever-changing circumstances of leadership and organizational challenges.

In its interactions with a richly varied client population, in its research into the effect of leadership on organizational performance and sustainability, and in its deep insight into the workings of organizations, CCL creates new, sound ideas that leaders all over the world put into action every day. We believe you will find the Ideas Into Action Guidebooks an important addition to your leadership toolkit.

Table of Contents

IN BRIEF

For a leader, having the ability to influence others is important. In nonprofit organizations leaders must successfully manage employees and volunteers, and maintain their commitment to the organizational mission. Leaders must also influence stakeholders, such as foundations, donors, and government agencies, which have control over the nonprofit's funding.

To successfully influence these various groups, you need to be aware of three influence outcomes: resistance, compliance, and commitment, with commitment being the most desired outcome. You also need to be aware of the various stakeholder groups for your organization, and how to adjust your influence tactics according to your audience. Finally, you need to learn how to use a variety of influence tactics, such as rational persuasion, consultation, inspirational appeals, and collaboration.

Next, you should complete a self-assessment of your current influence skills, and determine what areas you are strong in and what areas you need to develop. Then you can plan an influence session, where you determine what tactics you would use for a given audience, and put those tactics into place. Through self-awareness, skill building, planning, and successful execution, you can utilize influence as a means of achieving your nonprofit's goals.

Why Influence?

Influence is the power and ability to personally affect others' actions, decisions, opinions, or thoughts. As such, influence is an essential component of leadership, allowing leaders to promote ideas and to inspire people. Influence is important because it helps leaders achieve desirable outcomes, such as communicating a vision, aligning the efforts of others, building commitment to the mission and work, and expanding an organization's or a community's capacity to meet its challenges. Many leaders have influence in their organizations, but they are not always sure how best to use it.

In nonprofit organizations, influence is particularly important. Relationships are vital to a nonprofit's success. Leaders often use their influence to achieve results through staff members, volunteers, and other stakeholders. Nonprofit leaders don't always have the same tools as leaders in corporate enterprises, such as the resources to grant promotions or to reward teams and individuals with bonuses. Nonprofit staff and volunteers often consider their work not just a job but a passion and a commitment. The influence a leader practices can keep people motivated. If volunteers and staff lose faith in the nonprofit's mission and its leadership, they may not want to donate their time and energy to that cause and may seek opportunities elsewhere.

Influence in a nonprofit organization also helps to bring in and maintain funding to continue the nonprofit's work. Nonprofits are often dependent on various sources for funding. Leaders in these circumstances can use influence to encourage continued funding from foundations, individual and organizational donors, government agencies, and other sources. Whether for staff, volunteers, funders, or the public in general, nonprofit leaders need well-developed influence skills that encourage those groups to support the nonprofit's actions.

Nonprofit leaders who effectively influence others can achieve their goals and objectives more successfully than leaders who simply order people to do things. But what does it mean to effectively influence? To answer that question, you need to know that the use of influence skills or tactics can produce three distinctly different outcomes: resistance, compliance, and commitment. In *Leadership in Organizations*, Gary Yukl explains the differences between them.

Resistance

The least desirable outcome is resistance to the request you are making. People may directly oppose what you're asking for or resist in less direct ways, perhaps sabotaging your efforts to influence. For example, they may initially agree with your request, but then put roadblocks in the way of its completion or make excuses about why it cannot be accomplished.

> An organization is facing grim economic conditions on the horizon and extensive funding problems. The executive director decides to eliminate a department that, while once integral to the organization, has for some time brought diminishing returns and needs to be consolidated into another department to increase efficiency. The head of the department is a prized employee, and loyal members of the department resist the change, directly and indirectly sabotaging the executive director's efforts. Other members of the organization publicly agree that the department needs to be cut, but privately express disdain for the executive director's decision and are unwilling to cut and consolidate the department. In this situation, the executive director has been unable to influence members of this organization to carry out the request, and as a result has damaged some relationships and eroded trust.

Compliance

Compliance is better than resistance, and it is often the level of response you need to ensure that another person or group takes action in a desired way. Compliance is sufficient when your request is simple and routine and doesn't require the other person or group to exert much additional energy, resources, or effort to accomplish it. You can settle for compliance in such situations because your request isn't optional but required by the organization or by the team you lead.

Potential Outcomes of Influence Tactics

Commitment: Enthusiastic response with high-level effort
Compliance: Moderate response with minimal effort
Resistance: Minimal, if any, response with delayed effort

A new hire in a local nonprofit is charged with enforcing compliance with governmental regulations, something her predecessor failed to do. However, her staff is at first hesitant and resistant to these regulations, claiming that they are unnecessary and pointless. The new leader uses her influence skills to convince the staff that, like it or not, they must follow regulations, and though the staff remains somewhat unconvinced, they comply with the leader's request. This leader has used her influence to get compliance from her employees, which is all she needs to ensure that the organization adheres to regulations.

Commitment

When your influence efforts result in commitment, you have on your side voluntary endorsement and support for carrying out a task. This is an important distinction from compliance. Commitment is vital if what you ask requires other people to take on jobs that may not be simple, quick, or without cost to their personal time, work schedules, or budgets. When you are able to influence someone to the level of commitment, there are several advantages:

9

- There is greater sustained effort, which is particularly important when the tasks involved are complex or difficult and require a concentrated effort over a long period of time.

- Because committed people endorse your objectives, they tend to be more efficient, creative, resilient, and focused on your shared goal. Those efforts can often produce higher-quality work that goes beyond the minimum.

- Working relationships improve.

- There is less need to fight resistance.

A leader of a nonprofit decides to implement a new strategy to meet its goals and to accomplish its mission. Staff at the nonprofit are resistant to the changes, but the leader uses his influence skills to demonstrate how the changes will streamline the organization's processes and increase its capacity to serve its clients, which will greatly benefit the organization. Once they realize how the change will make their work better, members of the nonprofit become fully committed to the new strategy, and the nonprofit succeeds and flourishes. The leader has used his influence to receive full commitment from the staff, increasing the organization's efficiency and effectiveness.

Whom Do You Influence?

In the past, as you have tried to influence others—promoting a new idea, for example, or suggesting that things be done a different way—you have probably noticed that you use different approaches depending on the circumstances and on the result you want. The first step toward more successful influencing is to consider individual personalities, roles, goals, and objectives. Nonprofit leaders, like their corporate counterparts, are dependent on various stakeholder groups in order to be successful. Each stakeholder group has an interest in the outcome of decisions, how the work is done, who is included in the process, and other matters. Stakeholder groups have their own agendas, perspectives, and priorities. Sometimes they align with the leader's interests, and sometimes work is needed to create alignment and commitment.

Possible Stakeholder Groups

- legislative groups and federal, state, and local elected officials
- accreditation agencies
- donors
- employees and volunteers
- clients and others who receive the nonprofit's goods and services
- specialty groups (for example, potential employers of graduates of an educational institution)
- organizational partners
- marketplace and service competitors
- vendors
- foundations and philanthropic organizations

Influencing different stakeholder groups takes work. Sometimes you have to influence someone who occupies a more powerful position than you, or you have to influence a group whose main interest is different from yours. Sometimes you have to build partnerships with peers across community or organizational boundaries. And the challenge of motivating direct reports and volunteers is always present. You can't simply learn a set of rules for how to influence each of these groups, because each group operates in a different context and is likely to have different interests and preferences.

Influence works relationally. It's not just a matter of trading or bartering. If you use your influence only to trade favors, you may have some success, but it will be short-lived and subject to unanticipated changes. If you base your influence tactics on building relationships, you can create trust between yourself and your stakeholders that will help to sustain the relationship over time.

In addition to considering stakeholder interests, you should consider the kind of power relationship you share with your stakeholders. Two types of power are especially relevant: personal and positional. *Personal power* refers to the level of trust, respect, and relational commitment you share with another person or group. *Positional power* refers to the power associated with a title or a specific responsibility.

> As the head of operations for a nonprofit organization delivering medical services, Susan must meet with members of her organization and discuss some recent violations of confidentiality rules regarding client information. As these members have about the same rank as Susan, she is able to use her trust and respect in her colleagues to successfully communicate information about the importance of following the rules. Susan's colleagues, however, must communicate the information to their direct reports and are limited in the amount of information they can share about the violations. These colleagues are forced to use their authority to communicate successfully, because they may not be able to share information about the violations.

The Stakeholder Analysis Worksheet can help you think about which influence tactics you currently use or should use with different stakeholder groups. As you examine the grid, consider this question: How do your choice and use of influence tactics change with different groups? You can use the grid to record your own stakeholders. Stakeholders will fall into one of the five categories described below. Under each category, we have included possible strategies you can implement to increase your influence with those groups.

Allies agree with your thinking, strategy, and implementation plans. To increase your influence with allies:

- Acknowledge the quality of the relationship.

- Acknowledge the doubts and vulnerability that you have with respect to your vision and your project.

- Seek and use advice and support.

Opponents generally agree with your position, but disagree with your strategy and implementation plans. To increase your influence with opponents:

- Acknowledge the quality of the relationship and examine the assumption that it is based on trust.
- Clarify your position.
- Try to understand and remain neutral toward their perspective.
- Identify specific areas of disagreement and the underlying reasons for them—name the concerns, perceived risks, and assumptions.
- Strive for inclusive solutions.

Associates somewhat agree with your thinking, strategy, and implementation plans. To increase your influence with associates:

- Share information about what you are doing.
- Listen to what they are doing.
- Discuss how you might work together.
- Try to reach some agreement about how you are going to work together and help each other.

Adversaries distrust you and disagree with your thinking, strategy, and implementation plans. To increase your influence with adversaries:

- Listen to their point of view.
- Reflect on how you understand your adversary's position.
- Share your vision for your project.
- Discuss areas of disagreement and potential agreement.

People who are **undecided** may need more information before they can take a stand. They may be open to your influence. To increase your influence with those who are undecided:

- Share information about the work.
- Elicit their perspective.
- Share your perspective.
- Explore opportunities for working together and address concerns about working toward your goal.

Sometimes people treat opponents as if they are adversaries, so it is important to distinguish between these two categories. Just because there is disagreement with a person on a particular issue does not necessarily signal that there will be disagreement on a future issue. Trust is the critical attribute that helps to determine whether one should be regarded as an opponent or an adversary and, consequently, the methods of influence that you should use.

Influence Tactics

When you make a simple request, people are likely to carry it out provided that it does not negatively affect them. If your request is clearly legitimate, relevant to them or their role, and something they can do, resistance will probably be minimal. Selecting and developing a broader set of influence tactics becomes more important when your request is perceived as unpleasant, inconvenient, or inconsistent with their goals, values, or intentions. If it is not immediately obvious to other people that complying with your request is beneficial or necessary, it can be particularly difficult to influence their actions.

Table 1 lists influence tactics that research has identified as effective in different situations and with different people. In *Leadership in Organizations*, Gary Yukl divides eleven tactics into two groups: four core tactics that research suggests are most effective and most widely used, and seven supplementary tactics that leaders often use in conjunction with the core tactics.

Stakeholder Analysis Worksheet

Identify the stakeholders important to you, and map them onto the grid. Consider how your choice and use of influence tactics change with different groups.

High

	Associates	Allies
AGREEMENT		
	Adversaries	Opponents

Low   **TRUST**   High

Table 1. Proactive Influence Tactics

Core Influence Tactics

Rational persuasion	You use logical arguments and factual evidence to show that a request or proposal is feasible and relevant for attaining important task objectives.
Consultation	You ask the person to suggest improvements or help plan a proposed activity or change for which the person's support is desired.

15

Table 1. Proactive Influence Tactics (continued)

Inspirational appeals	You appeal to the person's values and ideals or seek to arouse the person's emotions to gain commitment for a request or proposal.
Collaboration	You offer to provide assistance or necessary resources if the person will carry out a request or approve a proposed change.

Supplementary Influence Tactics

Apprising	You explain how carrying out a request or supporting a proposal will benefit the person or his or her organization or cause.
Ingratiation	You use praise and flattery before or during an attempt to influence the target person to carry out a request or support a proposal.
Exchange	You offer something the person wants, or offer to reciprocate at a later time, if the person will do what you ask.
Personal appeals	You ask the person to carry out a request or support a proposal as a personal favor based on friendship or the person's kindness.
Legitimating	You seek to establish the legitimacy of a request or to verify that you have the authority to make the request.
Pressure	You use demands, threats, frequent checking, or persistent reminders to influence the person to do something.
Coalition	You enlist the support of others to help you in influencing the person, or you use their endorsement of your request or proposal in your influence attempt.

Which Influence Tactics Do You Use?

Pay attention to which of the influence tactics in Table 1 you use most often and which ones you seldom use. You may be overusing or underusing various tactics. Being able to effectively use different tactics can help prepare you to use your influence more effectively with different kinds of stakeholders and in different situations.

Research reveals that the four primary influence tactics are the most effective for creating commitment. If you are adept at these tactics, you will probably be successful in influencing others.

To assess the influence tactics you currently use, complete the Your Use of Core Influence Tactics Worksheet. Granted, this simple self-assessment is not a rigorous, empirical examination of your use of influence tactics or an inventory of how people practice influence in your organization. But if you round out your self-assessment by asking others for their impressions and observations of how you influence, you can use all of that information to get a practical sense of what tactics you can use more often and which ones you can rein in. If you find that you want to improve your use of certain tactics, practice in low-risk situations and find a role model (someone who is adept in the tactic) to help you measure your progress.

Your Use of Core Influence Tactics Worksheet

Place a check mark in the cell with the best response for each of the statements below. As you respond to the statements, think about how you typically approach making a request of a person or group. Although your choice of influence tactics can depend on whom, why, where, and when you influence, this exercise is intended to provide a general sense of the tactics you typically use.

		Almost never	Sometimes	Almost always
1	I explain the reason for the requested action.			
2	I offer factual evidence that the proposal is needed and feasible.			

		Almost never	Sometimes	Almost always
3	I ask for ideas about how to carry out the requested action and incorporate those ideas into the process.			
4	I thoughtfully respond to concerns and suggestions.			
5	I show how the requested action furthers goals and values held by the person with whom I am speaking.			
6	I link my request to a vision the person can fully support.			
7	I provide the necessary resources (time, staff, materials, technical support, etc.) to accomplish the task.			
8	I reduce the difficulty of carrying out the request by removing barriers to success.			

Items 1 and 2 are examples of rational persuasion.
Items 3 and 4 are examples of consultation.
Items 5 and 6 are examples of inspirational appeals.
Items 7 and 8 are examples of collaboration.

Review which of these four influence tactics you tend to use most and least. How well have these tactics worked for you? Are there any tactics you may be overusing or underusing?

The first step toward more successful influencing is to consider individual personalities, roles, goals, and objectives.

Conducting an Influence Session

So far, we have discussed tailoring your influence strategy to the particular person from whom you seek support and broadening your tactical choices by assessing which tactics you tend to use more than others. Another aspect of influence you may need to account for is the situation in which you use it. To use influence most effectively, you need to read the situation, see how the other person fits in it, and then decide which tactic will serve you best and when you should apply it.

One way you can seize the right moment to use an influence tactic is to carefully plan each situation in which you plan to solicit the support of others. Clearly, you cannot plan for every contingency, and sometimes the opportunity to exercise influence arises unexpectedly. But planning will help you think through different contingencies, develop responses to how others might receive your influence, and imagine alternative tactics so that you can switch to one that, in the moment, may be more effective.

Create your plan in the form of a script in which you describe what you are trying to accomplish and assess the stakeholders from whom you seek endorsement and support. You can also review the influence tactics you tend to favor and those you often avoid using. Imagine the situation and anticipate what kind of reaction you are likely to get. After developing such a plan, you can then map the details of a meeting with the person or group you need to influence. Using the information in the following sections, think through the actions you will take before and during an influence session. After the session, review your actions and the responses of the person you were trying to influence. Reflect on your efforts so that you can learn from your experience and use what you learn to shape future encounters.

Setting Your Influence Goals

You are more likely to have success influencing others if you establish clear goals, assess your audience, identify appropriate influence tactics, and practice using them. Answering all or some of the following questions can help you work out your thoughts on whom you need to influence and what you want or need to accomplish.

- Whom or which group are you attempting to influence, and what position does that person or group occupy relative to yours?

- What is the situation? Has your organization assigned you this task? How much support do you need?

- Why did you choose to initiate your request? Why do you need this person's or this group's support for your idea?

- What do you want the outcome of your influence session to be? Will compliance suffice, or do you need commitment?

- What benefits will you and the person or group you want to influence receive if you handle the situation well? What will it cost you and the person or group you want to influence to deal effectively with the situation?

- Assess the differences and similarities of personal and positional power between yourself and the person or group you want to influence. How can you leverage this power to increase your influence?

- What influence tactics should you choose to drive, accelerate, and implement change in your organization?

- Which tactics do you need to start using or use more often?

- Which tactics do you need to use less or stop using?

Identifying Benefits and Challenges

Each time you exercise influence, subsequent attempts to influence can become easier or more difficult. For example, you may have had a negative confrontation in the past with the person or group you are now hoping to influence. How will you deal with the residual effect of that confrontation? On the positive side, perhaps the organization recognizes that you have some expertise in a particular area and the person or group you want to influence wants to gain some expertise in that area as well. By identifying these kinds of benefits and challenges, you can capitalize on positive aspects associated with the influence session and address its challenges. You can also increase your chances of successfully influencing the person. Use the Influence Benefits and Challenges Worksheet to determine the obstacles or challenges that exist in influencing the person, to highlight benefits or other positive aspects that you can use to increase your chances of success, and to capture specific action items to consider. We have highlighted three broad areas that often connect with benefits and challenges: relationship, politics and power, and skills and knowledge. You may think of other areas in which benefits and challenges exist.

Developing Your Influence Session Script

Given what you know about the situation and the person or group you want to influence, describe in detail how a conversation

might go. Successfully influencing another person or group involves more than just making a request. To gain commitment, you want to engage at a more substantial level— communicating your goal, explaining the benefits of joining your effort, and securing the other person's or the group's endorsement.

Start describing your planned scenario by using the influence tactics that are likely to work best given what you know. Review Table 1 to choose tactics you think would be the most effective. Then turn to your assessment of your influence tactics skills. Review how you

21

Influence Benefits and Challenges Worksheet

Influence Categories	Benefits (Positive Factors)	Challenges (Negative Factors)	Potential Next Steps
Relationship What kind of working relationship do you have with the person or group you want to influence? What level of trust and respect exists? Have you worked cooperatively in the past? Was that work successful? What made it successful? Have you had or do you have a conflict with this person or group? What situation led to the conflict? Was the conflict resolved? Are there lingering repercussions?			
Politics and Power Does the person or group you want to influence have a more or less powerful position than you? How might that difference affect your influence strategy?			

22

Influence Benefits and Challenges Worksheet (continued)

Influence Categories	Benefits (Positive Factors)	Challenges (Negative Factors)	Potential Next Steps
Skills and Knowledge Does the person or group you want to influence possess skills and knowledge that would help accomplish your goal or contribute to your proposal? Would helping you achieve your goal gain the person or group recognition? Does your vision encroach on the person or group's domain?			

Based on your analysis, is your attempt to influence this person in this situation likely to result in a positive outcome?

scored yourself on the Your Use of Core Influence Tactics Worksheet. Pay particular attention to the tactics that you use less frequently, and think about how you can develop them before your influence session to increase your chance of success.

It may not take a lot of work to develop tactics that you haven't used much before. For example, you may be skilled with using logical arguments and factual evidence to persuade someone or to make a request. Perhaps the person or group you want to influence is known for being generous or creative more than analytical. In that case, you can look at your proposal in terms of how it inspires or arouses enthusiasm by appealing to values and ideals.

Another way to develop your underused influence tactics is to evaluate the benefits you have identified and think about how you can use them to shore up seldom-used tactics. For example, if you are skilled at collaborating but find creating a logical rationale a challenge, perhaps you can reach out to others to help you develop a logical argument. Developing some tactics to the level you need to be an effective influencer may require more practice, coaching, or research. Your goal before starting an influence session is to have confidence in and comfort with the tactics you have chosen to use. Use the Influence Session Worksheet to work through your plan.

Conducting an Influence Session

After you have assessed your influence-tactics preferences, described your goals, described the person or group you are trying to influence, and sketched the groundwork for your influence session, you are ready to meet with the person or group you want to influence. Use the ideas you developed in your Influence Session Worksheet to help you stay focused on your goal during the conversation. Interpersonal and communication skills are critical at this stage, and you can enhance both by setting the stage for your request and by establishing a rapport.

Set the stage. Pick the right time and place for your influence session. Find a setting where there will be minimal distractions. Pick a neutral site to minimize personal and positional power differences.

Create an atmosphere that encourages openness, optimism, and connection. Positional power may be needed (such as the higher-ranking person's office) if the best you can hope for in a situation is compliance.

Establish a rapport. Describe the situation. Check to see that there is understanding by asking clarifying questions to clear up any confusion, to define problems, to uncover gaps in information, and to encourage accuracy and precision. Be mindful of the impact of your nonverbal communication—body language and tone of voice. Make sure to establish eye contact, smile, and indicate that you appreciate being listened to. Watch for reactions to what you say, and build on points of agreement to create momentum toward the outcome you want.

Reflecting on Your Influence Session

To increase your influence skills, learn from your experiences. Each time you attempt to influence, even just to make a small request, take the opportunity to think back over the encounter and how you adjusted your techniques and tactics or chose other tactics altogether. The following questions can guide your learning from experience:

- What went well during the session? Describe the situation and the person's or group's response.

- What did not go well? Describe the situation and the person's or group's response.

- Did you get the outcome you wanted? Describe any compromises or modifications to your intended goal.

- What steps did you and the person or group agree to take next?

- What did you learn about yourself and your ability to influence others?

- What would you do differently next time?

- What additional support can you find to develop your influence skills?

Influence Session Worksheet

Which influence tactics are likely to be most effective?

What specifically will you say and do to use these tactics?

Anticipate possible responses. What is the person's or group's likely reaction to what you are proposing? What might the person or group say or think?

Influence Session Worksheet (continued)

Create your counterargument. Plan how you are going to use additional influence tactics to reply, if necessary, to the response.

Identify potential points of mutual agreement and use them to move toward your desired outcome. Secure agreement on your desired outcome. Establish clear steps that both of you will take to accomplish your agreed-upon goals and a timeline for doing them.

End on a positive note. Express your appreciation and communicate your willingness to meet again to check on the progress being made toward the goal.

Conclusion

Influencing others is not easy, especially if you do not have direct authority to back up your request. As a leader in a nonprofit organization, that is often the case. Nonprofit leaders deal with many different stakeholders, from foundations to volunteers to governmental agencies to clients and their constituencies. Even if you have authority to make a request, gaining commitment takes more skill than getting compliance. During your service as a nonprofit leader, you will draw on your skills as an influencer again and again. Your ability to influence others depends not just on your learning and practicing different tactics. The thoughtful use of tactics is just part of what can be a complex interaction that plays out differently at different levels of the organization and among different people. Achieving results by influencing others can also include the following factors:

- a reputation of trustworthiness, credibility, and flexibility
- communication and relationship skills
- a focus on creating broad, shared benefits
- an ability to identify with the interests of others
- avoiding being perceived as manipulative or selfish
- an ability to read situational cues such as body language or the setting you are in (a formal office or over lunch, for example)

Influencing someone to endorse an agenda or to commit to goals may not happen immediately. Each individual or group you attempt to influence has to carefully consider the costs and benefits involved. This guidebook touches on but one aspect of influence—tactics. Nonprofit leaders at all levels should be well versed in these tactics and their use. On a broader scale, influence emerges as a multi-faceted, relational, power-shifting, and collaborative enterprise. Differences—in culture, age, gender, role, and motive, for example—can complicate your role as a leader and how you influence others. In all of its aspects, influence frames direction, alignment, and commitment among individuals, groups, and organizations. It stakes out significant ground in strategy, transformation, and innovation, among other spaces.

The importance of influence for nonprofit organizations cannot be understated. Effectively using influence allows you to further your nonprofit's mission in a variety of ways. For instance, as a nonprofit leader, you most likely regularly interact with many different kinds of people with varied interests and backgrounds. Knowing how to tailor your influence tactics to best reach a specific audience goes a long way to ensure that you influence successfully. To serve well as a leader in a nonprofit, become aware of how to effectively reach the people and the groups that have a stake in your organization's future. Using the tactics and skills outlined in this guidebook will help.

The response you get to your influence efforts will test your flexibility and adaptability as a leader, and will shape your expectations for future encounters. Learning how to get results with others is a long-term, ongoing process—just like many other aspects of leadership.

Background

Research about how managers use influence has a long history and has led to the understanding that leaders can use multiple tactics to build commitment and get results from peers, direct reports, and bosses.

CCL identifies influence as one of four fundamental leader competencies (ranked with self-awareness, learning agility, and communication). Influence emerges in different ways in many of CCL's programs: in assessment instruments, in videotaped role-plays, and in scripted vignettes. Influence also plays a supporting role in several of CCL's Ideas Into Action Guidebooks, reinforcing ideas such as networking among leaders; broaching new ideas in organizations; sharing the accomplishments of your team and yourself; and communicating a vision to groups, teams, and organizations.

CCL first published a guidebook about influence tactics in 2004. Since then, CCL has continued to develop notions about influence and move beyond tactics. Even so, the subject of influence tactics—what they are, which ones are effective, which ones are most used—remains important to leaders. A revised second edition (2011) puts the idea of influence tactics in a shared space with other aspects of influence. CCL believes that the practices discussed in that edition constitute one important point in a constellation of its knowledge about influence. It plans to publish more on that topic—including this edition, adapted for leaders of nonprofit organizations—in order to articulate for its clients and the public a range of influence practices that emerge at different levels of leadership responsibility.

Suggested Resources

Carnegie, D. (1982). *How to win friends and influence people* (Rev. ed.). New York, NY: Pocket Books.

Gardner, H. (2004). *Changing minds: The art and science of changing our own and other people's minds.* Boston, MA: Harvard Business School Press.

Goldstein, N. J., Martin, S. J., & Cialdini, R. B. (2010). *Yes! 50 scientifically proven ways to be persuasive.* New York, NY: Free Press.

Scharlatt, H. (2008). *Selling your ideas to your organization.* Greensboro, NC: Center for Creative Leadership.

Yukl, G. (2007). Best practices in the use of proactive influence tactics by leaders. In J. Conger & R. Riggio (Eds.), *The practice of leadership* (pp. 109–128). San Francisco, CA: Jossey-Bass.

Yukl, G. (2010). *Leadership in organizations* (7th ed.). Upper Saddle River, NJ: Pearson Education.

Ordering Information

TO GET MORE INFORMATION, TO ORDER OTHER IDEAS INTO ACTION GUIDEBOOKS, OR TO FIND OUT ABOUT BULK-ORDER DISCOUNTS, PLEASE CONTACT US BY PHONE AT 336-545-2810 OR VISIT OUR ONLINE BOOKSTORE AT WWW.CCL.ORG/GUIDEBOOKS.

CPSIA information can be obtained
at www.ICGtesting.com
Printed in the USA
BVOW11s2054290316

442222BV00007B/8/P